AF316805

# LUCAS SHARES WITH LIAM

# Lucas Shares with Liam

## Book Two

Jessica Adams

LLJA Adventures Publishing

Published by LLJA Adventures Publishing LLC
Graphics by Jessica Brook Adams

First Printing, 2024

# LUCAS AND LIAM LEARN TOGETHER SERIES

BOOK ONE: LUCAS MEETS LIAM

BOOK TWO: LUCAS SHARES WITH LIAM

COMING SOON!

BOOK THREE: LUCAS AND LIAM LEARN TO COOK

# DEDICATION

Dedication

To my stars in the night
on an unlit, but new path
Lighting my way down this unbeaten path


This is a story of fiction. Although some people were used as models to make the graphics, this is not a retelling of real events.

My name


My siblings name(s)

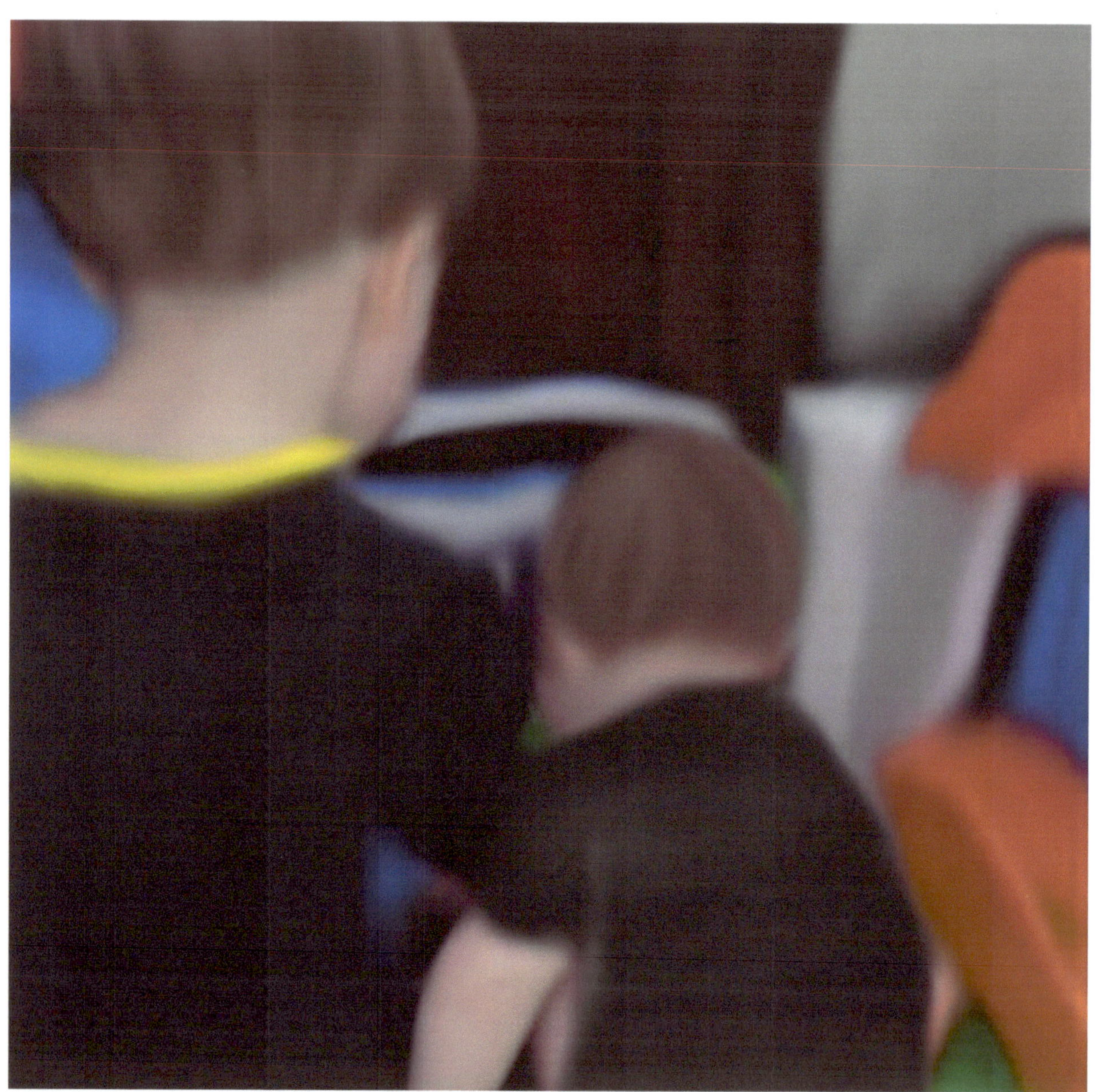

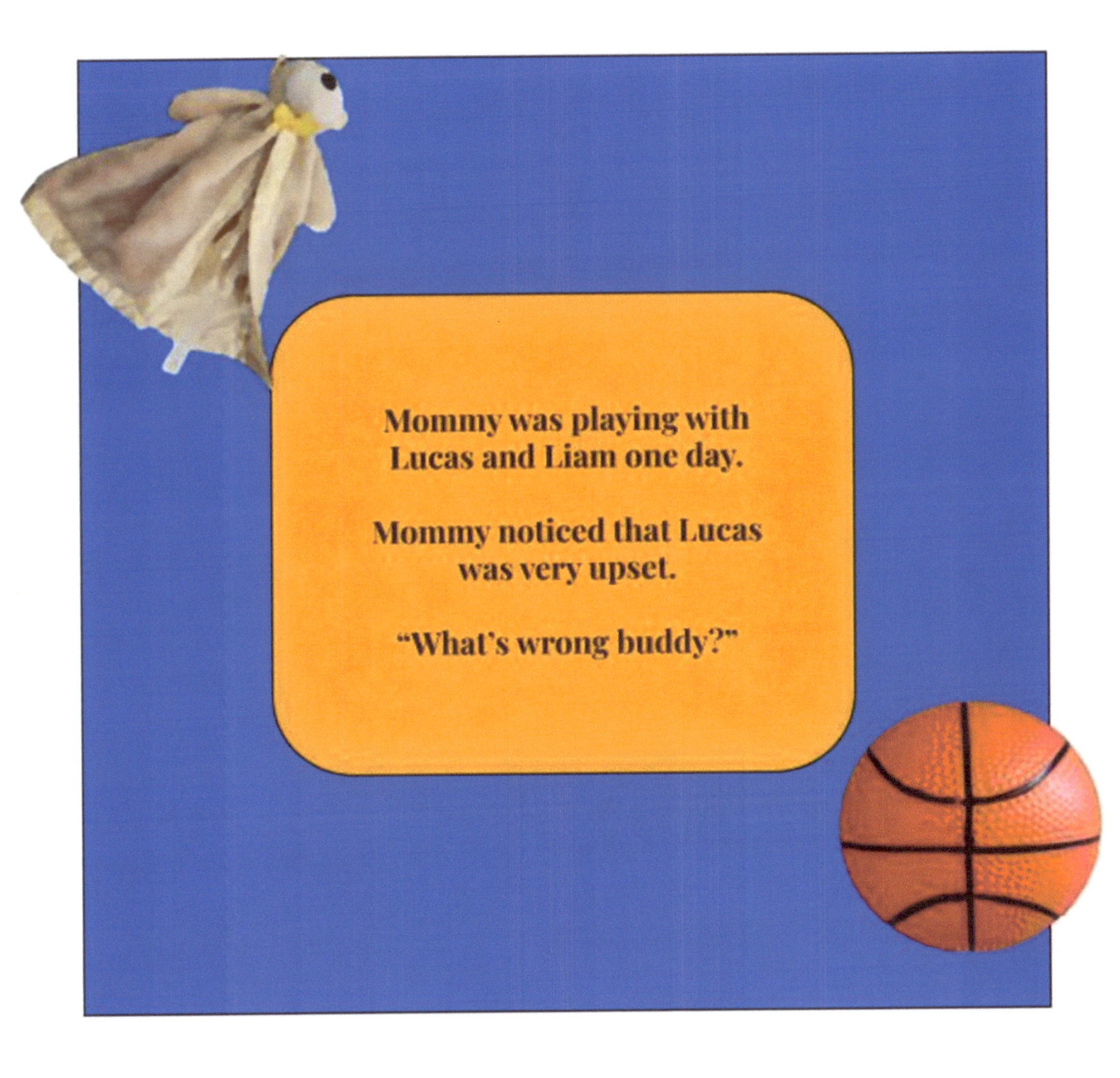
Mommy was playing with
Lucas and Liam one day.

Mommy noticed that Lucas
was very upset.

"What's wrong buddy?"

"I don't want you to play with brother. I just want you to spend time with me. He always messes up my toys!"

Lucas continued to pout.

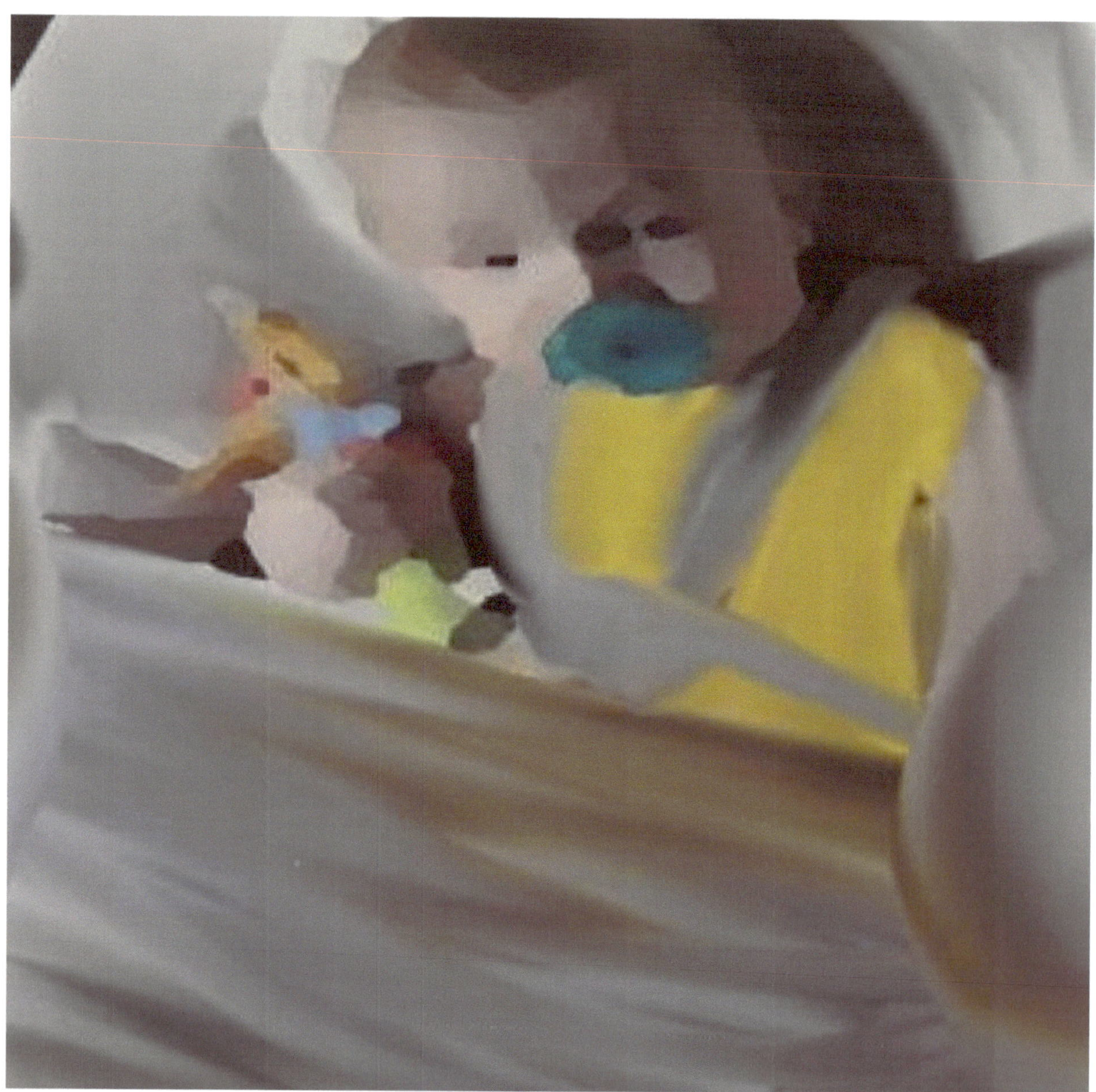

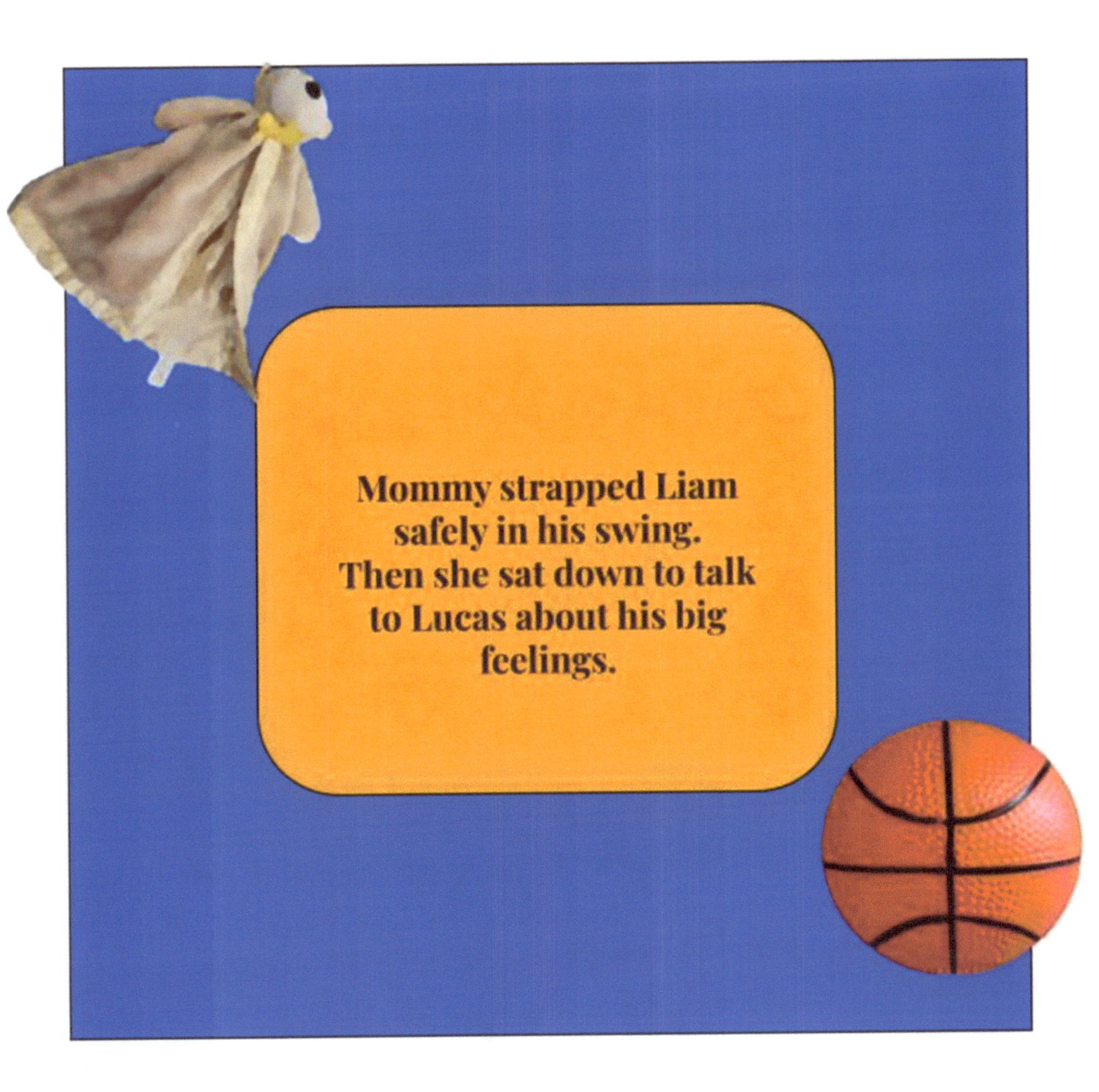

Mommy strapped Liam
safely in his swing.
Then she sat down to talk
to Lucas about his big
feelings.

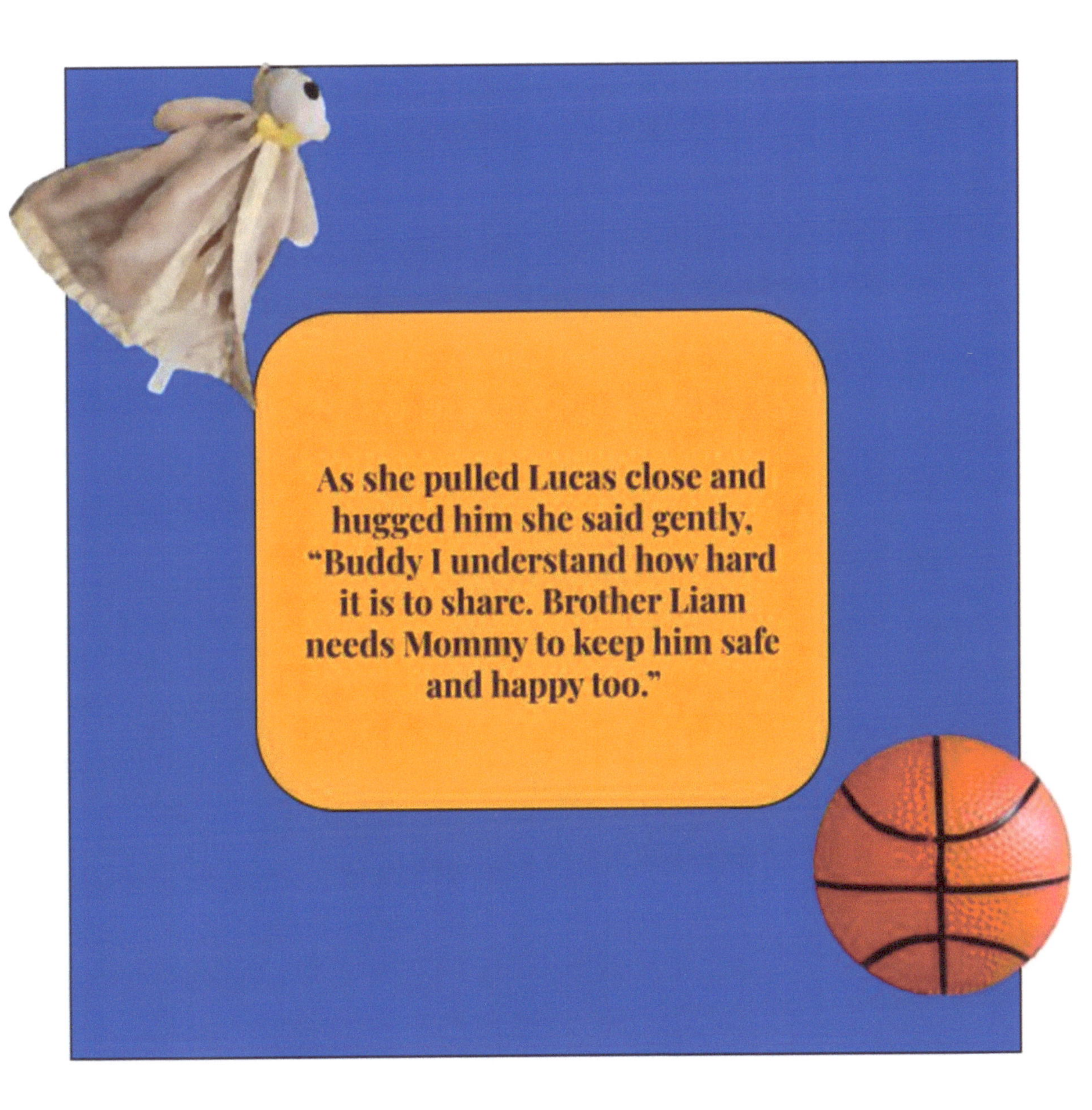

As she pulled Lucas close and
hugged him she said gently,
"Buddy I understand how hard
it is to share. Brother Liam
needs Mommy to keep him safe
and happy too."

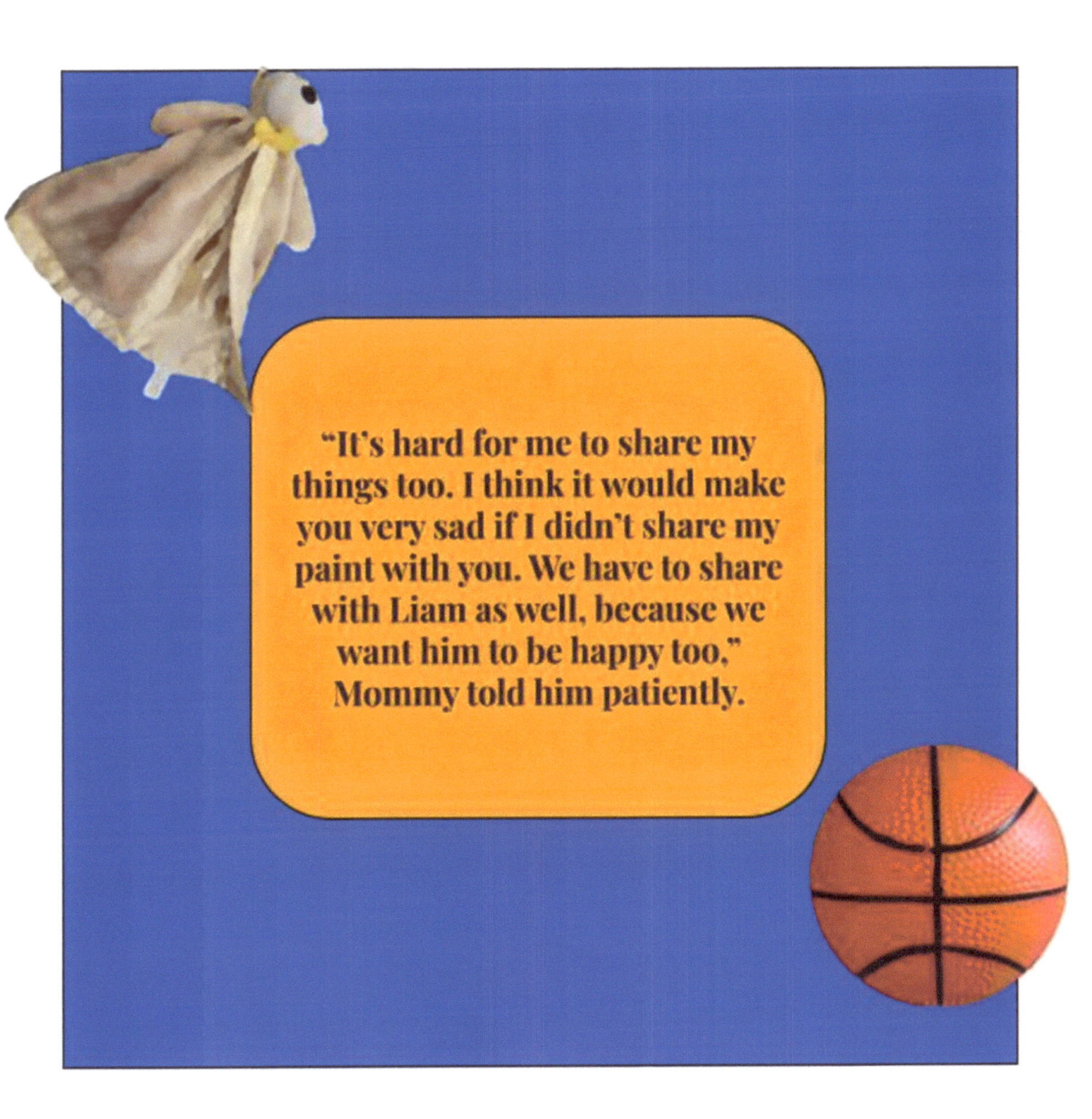
"It's hard for me to share my things too. I think it would make you very sad if I didn't share my paint with you. We have to share with Liam as well, because we want him to be happy too," Mommy told him patiently.

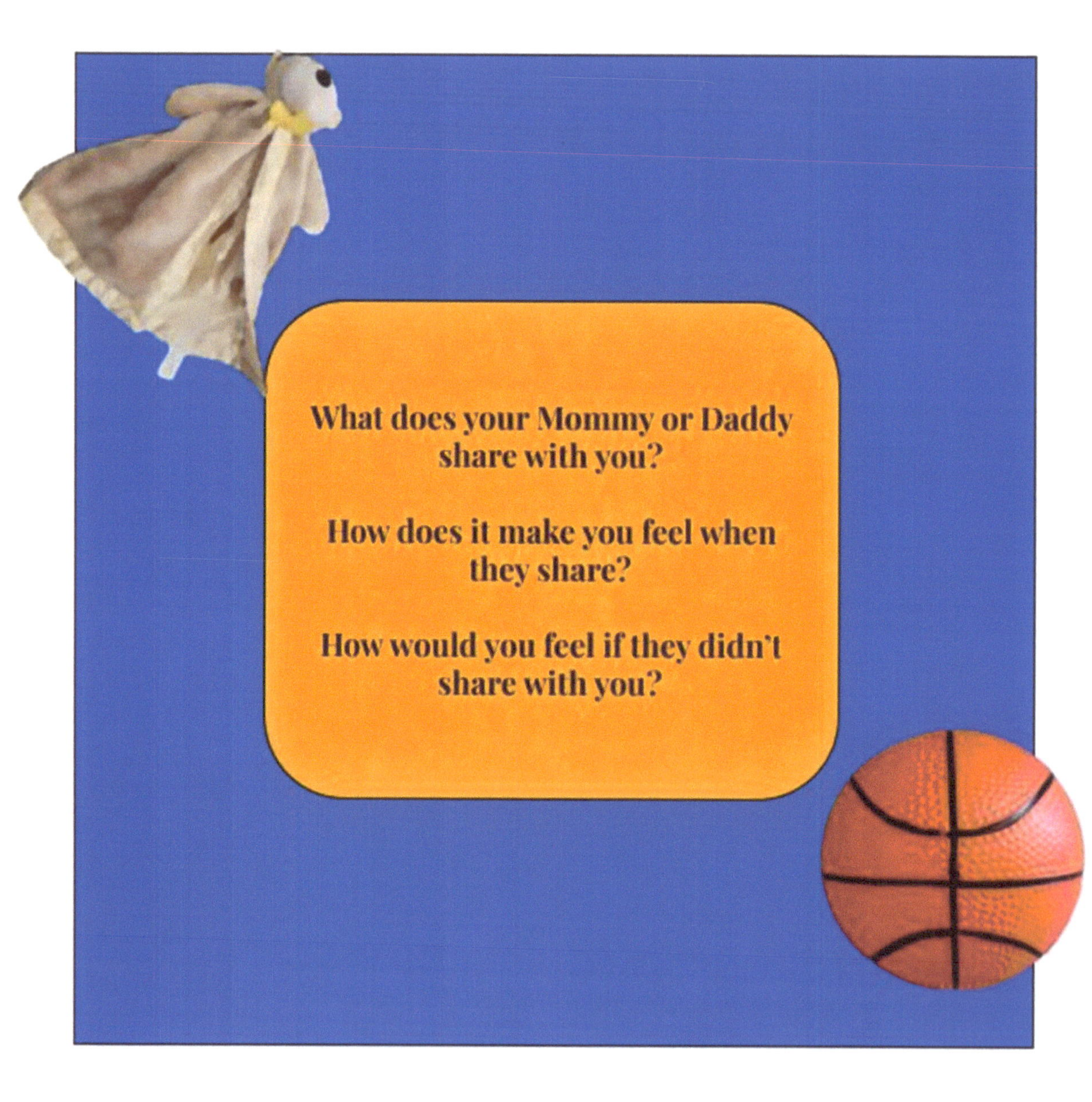
What does your Mommy or Daddy
share with you?

How does it make you feel when
they share?

How would you feel if they didn't
share with you?

Picture of someone
sharing with me.

Lucas thought hard about what Mommy told him.

How would he feel if Mommy never shared with him?

That's how brother Liam would feel, if Lucas never shared.

Later, Lucas came out of
his room with his doctor
coat and all of his
equipment.

"Hello, Doctor Lucas. What brings you here today?" Mommy asked.

Lucas used his doctor voice, "Liam does not look good. I am here to make sure he is happy again."

Mommy giggled, "Thank you so much doctor."

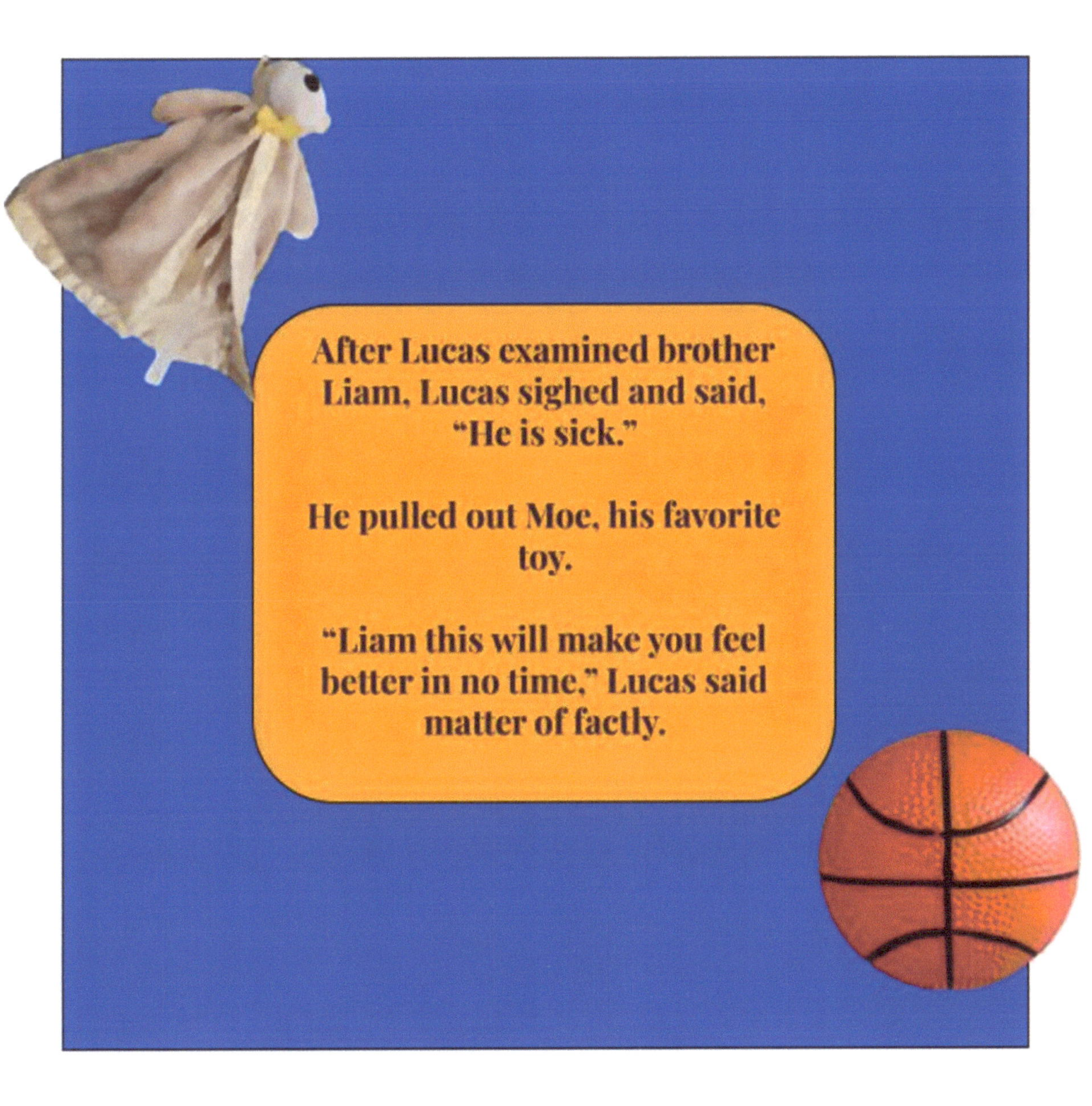


After Lucas examined brother Liam, Lucas sighed and said, "He is sick."

He pulled out Moe, his favorite toy.

"Liam this will make you feel better in no time," Lucas said matter of factly.

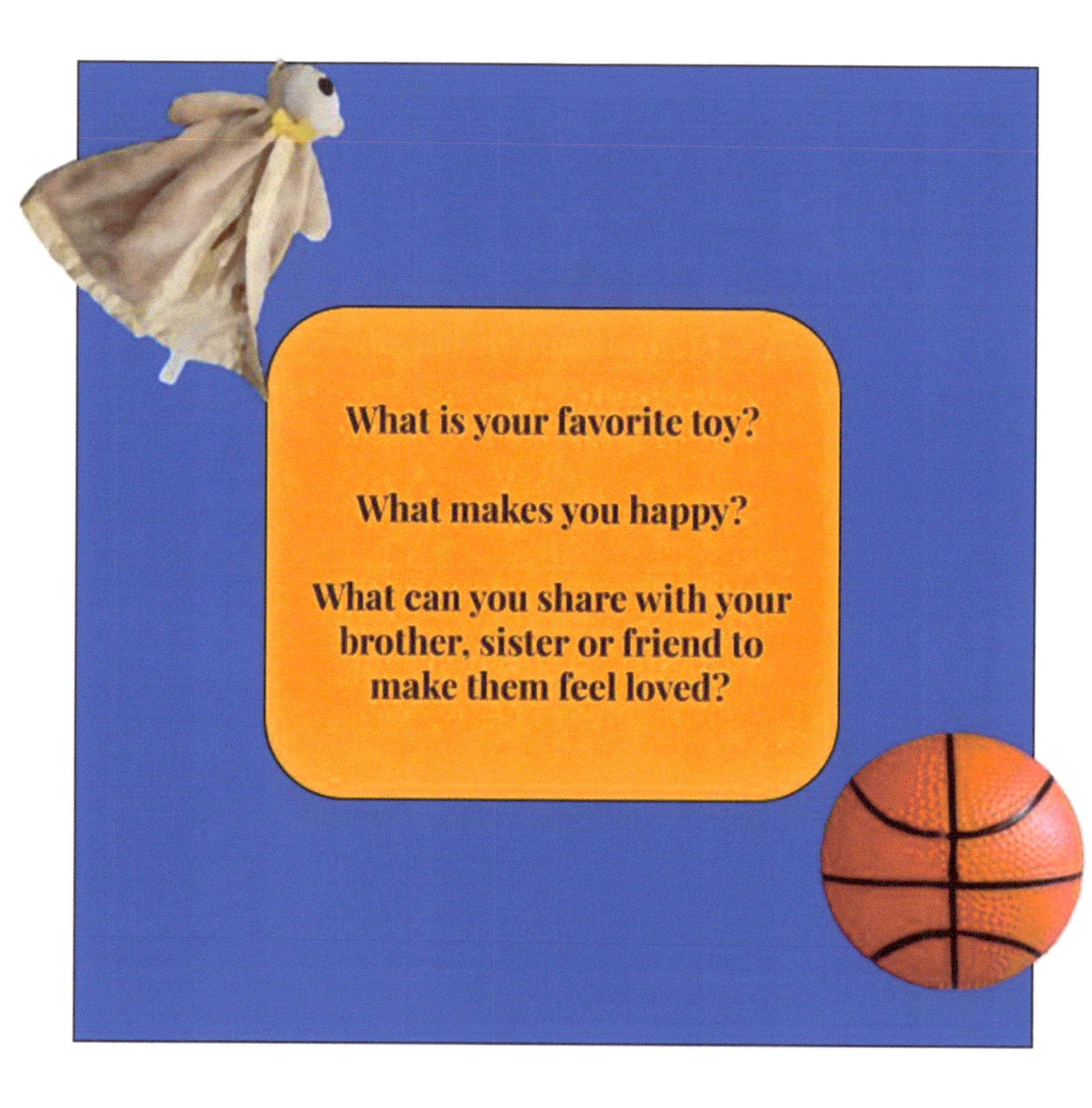

What is your favorite toy?

What makes you happy?

What can you share with your brother, sister or friend to make them feel loved?

Here's a picture of me
sharing my favorite toy.

# ABOUT AUTHOR

Adams has loved the written word her whole life. There is just something special about holding a physical book and reading it. Literature remains through the years the biggest gift the world has. She hopes to work with youth one day using books to change lives and prevent mental health struggles from developing into adulthood.

She continues to work on service projects to fight against violence in communities.